A Rookie reader®

Jordan's Silly Sick Day

Written by Justine Fontes
Illustrated by Jared Lee

Children's Press®
A Division of Scholastic Inc.
New York • Toronto • London • Auckland • Sydney
Mexico City • New Delhi • Hong Kong
Danbury, Connecticut

To Leahbelle and her little ones, Jordan and Laurel, in the fond
hope that you'll be more often silly than sick.
—J.F.

To Kent and Jennifer
—J.L.

Reading Consultants

Linda Cornwell
Literacy Specialist

Katharine A. Kane
Education Consultant
(Retired, San Diego County Office of Education and San Diego State University)

Library of Congress Cataloging-in-Publication Data

Fontes, Justine.
  Jordan's silly sick day / written by Justine Fontes ; illustrated by Jared Lee.
      p. cm. — (A rookie reader)
  Summary: While sick in bed, a young boy is bored until he begins to use his imagi-
nation and soon he realizes that he feels better.
  ISBN 0-516-25897-4 (lib. bdg.)   0-516-26821-X (pbk.)
  [1. Sick–Fiction. 2. Imagination–Fiction.] I. Lee, Jared D., ill. II. Title. III. Series.
  PZ7.F73576Jo 2004
  [E]–dc22

                                                    2003016585

CHILDREN'S PRESS, and A ROOKIE READER®, and associated logos are trademarks
and or registered trademarks of Scholastic Library Publishing. SCHOLASTIC and
associated logos are trademarks and or registered trademarks of Scholastic Inc.
1 2 3 4 5 6 7 8 9 10 R 13 12 11 10 09 08 07 06 05 04

I am sick. That's no fun!

I can't play outside.
I can't see my friends.

I am wheezing
and sneezing.

The worst part of staying home is being bored!

Then I remember something.
I can use my imagination!

I pretend my Teddy bear
can play cards.

I let Teddy win.

I try to build a house of cards.
Then I wonder.

What if I lived in a real house
of cards?

A monster blows down my house!

So I build a house of blocks.

The monster kicks down my house of blocks.

So I build a house of books.

That stops the monster,
because he can't read.

I take a sip of orange juice.

I pretend I'm floating down
an orange river.

I can't be in school with my friends today.

But I sure am having lots of fun.

What shall I imagine next?

I imagine I am feeling better.

Guess what? It's working!

Word List (83 words)

a	friends	my	staying
am	fun	next	stops
an	guess	no	sure
and	having	of	take
be	he	orange	Teddy
bear	home	outside	that
because	house	part	that's
being	I	play	the
better	I'm	pretend	then
blocks	if	read	to
blows	imagination	real	
books	imagine	r...	
bored	in		use
build	i...	...ool	what
but		see	wheezing
can		shall	win
can't	kicks	sick	...ith
cards	let	sip	wonder
down	lived	sneezing	working
feeling	lots	so	worst
floating	monster	something	

About the Author
Justine Fontes and her husband, Ron, hope to write 1,001 terrific tales.
So far, they have penned nearly 400 children's books! They live in a quiet
corner of Maine with three happy cats.

About the Illustrator
Jared Lee was raised in Van Buren, Indiana. He has lived in Lebanon, Ohio,
for over thirty years, where he draws funny things all the live long day.